WEIRD WILDLIFE

MAMMALS

Jen Green

Raintree

Chicago, Illinois

LOOK FOR THE ELEPHANT

Look for the elephant in boxes like this. Here you will find extra facts, stories, and other interesting information about mammals.

▼ Gorillas live in the tropical forests of Central Africa. Find out more about them on page 24.

Published by Raintree, a division of Reed Elsevier, Inc.

Designer: Katrina Fiske
Editors: Cathy Grant, Pam Wells
Consultant: Joyce Pope

Library of Congress Cataloging-in-Publication Data
Green, Jen.
   Mammals / Jen Green.
      p. cm.
   Summary: Provides an overview to the variety, distribution, habits, physical characteristics, and more of mammals.

   ISBN 0-7398-4856-9 (HC),
   1-4109-0078-9 (Pbk.)
   1. Mammals—Juvenile literature.
[1. Mammals.] I. Title.

QL706.2 .G74 2002
599—dc21   2001034938

Printed in Hong Kong.
1 2 3 4 5 6 7 8 9 0 LB 05 04 03 02 01

J13Acknowledgments
We wish to thank the following individuals and organizations for their help and assistance and for supplying material in their collections: Bruce Coleman Collection 12 top (Joe McDonald), 17 top (Antonio Manzanares), 22 (Jen & Des Bartlett); Corbis 4 (Kevin Schafer), 5 top (Gallo Images/Nigel J Dennis), 5 (Kevin Schafer), 6 top (Galen Rowell), 8 top (Michael & Patricia Fogden), 9 (Keren Su), 10 bottom Su), 27 (Tom Brakefield), 28 (Tom Brakefield); FLPA 6 bottom (Dembinsky), 7 (Gerard Lacz), 10 top (Gerard Lacz)(Wolfgang Kaehler), 11 (Joe McDonald), 12 bottom (The Purcell Team), 14 (Randy Wells), 15 left (Gallo Images/Nigel J Dennis), 15 Right (Yann Arthus-Bertrand), 17 bottom (Lynda Richardson), 18 bottom (Karl Ammann), 21 (Tom Brakefield), 23 top (Tom Brakefield), 25 (Keren , 13 (Gerard Lacz), 18 top (E Schuiling), 20 top (Minden Pictures), 20 bottom (Silvestris), 26 (Winifried Wisniewski); MPM Images 1, 2, 3, 8 bottom, 16, 23 bottom, 24; NHPA 30 (Roger Tidman), 31 (Gerard Lacz); Oxford Scientific Films 19 (Rudie H Kuiter), 29 (David M Dennis).

CONTENTS

▶ These strange-looking mammals are called manatees. Find out more on page 8.

The Weird World of Mammals

Animals as different as whales, elephants, and mice have one vital thing in common. They are all mammals—members of one of the main groups of animals on Earth.

▲ Some mammals, like this beluga whale, spend their whole lives in water.

The mammal group includes many weird and wonderful creatures. Scaly armadillos, spiky porcupines, long-nosed tapirs, and night-loving bats are all part of this family of animals. There are about 4,000 different kinds of mammals. People are mammals, too.

Mammals vary a lot in size. Blue whales are the largest mammals. A big blue whale weighs 25 times as much as the largest land mammal, the African elephant. The hefty elephant weighs as much as 100 adult people. The world's smallest mammal is Kitti's hog-nosed bat, which has a body the size of a bumblebee!

▶ Apes and monkeys, like proboscis monkeys, belong to a group of mammals called primates. Humans belong to the same group.

LIVE YOUNG

Most mammal mothers give birth to fully formed babies, rather than laying eggs like birds and reptiles. Babies feed on their mother's milk. Adult mammals look after their young and may teach them the skills they need in life.

◀ Many mammal babies stay with their parents for months or even years. Young aardvarks drink their mother's milk for four months.

Mammals Everywhere

Mammals can be found all over the world: on dry land, in ponds and streams, and in the oceans. Bats spend part of their lives in the air and monkeys swing through the treetops. Moles live underground.

▲ Llamas live high in the Andes Mountains in South America. Their thick, fine fur keeps them warm in the icy winds.

On land, mammals are found in tropical jungles, pine forests, grasslands, and even high in the mountains. Sheep, cows, and horses are mammals that have been tamed so they can live and work with humans. Dogs and cats share our homes as pets. But most mammals run wild!

◀ The strange-looking star-nosed mole makes its home in an underground burrow. This strong swimmer finds its food in ponds and streams.

CITY DWELLERS

Mammals such as foxes, raccoons, and rats make their homes in crowded cities. They mostly hide by day and come out to look for food at night. When we are asleep, they search through our garbage to find food scraps.

▶ **Elephant seals spend most of their lives in the oceans. But they come ashore to breed on rocky beaches. Only the males have swollen snouts that look like elephants' trunks.**

Mammals are warm-blooded. Surprisingly, their body temperature stays about the same even when it is very cold or hot. This means that mammals can survive in harsh places such as icy Arctic wastes and hot, dry deserts. However, keeping an even body temperature uses up lots of energy, so mammals need to eat a lot of food.

Inside and Out

All mammals have a bony skeleton, though their bodies may be large or small and come in many different shapes. All mammals also have hair covering their bodies, though some don't have very much!

Mammals have similar bodies, however large or small they are. Land mammals all have four limbs, and most have a tail, though humans do not. Dolphins and whales look a lot like fish, but they are also mammals. Their front limbs have developed into flippers, and their back legs have disappeared completely. Their smooth, tapering shape helps them swim through the water easily.

▲ The kinkajou uses its tail as an extra limb to hang onto branches. Other mammals use their tails to flick away flies or to balance when running along tree branches.

◄ Manatees are mammals that dwell in water, like seals, whales, and dolphins. They swim along by beating their powerful tails up and down.

The hair on mammals' bodies helps them to keep warm. In cold weather, the hairs stand up to trap a layer of warm air next to the skin. The musk oxen of the Arctic have the longest hair of any mammal. Mammals that live in cold places, such as seals and whales, have an extra layer of fat, called blubber, under their skin. This keeps them warm even in icy water and snow.

▼ All mammals groom or clean their fur to keep it in good condition. Macaque monkeys help one another by removing ticks and fleas.

HIBERNATION

Some mammals survive the winter cold by falling into an amazing deep sleep called hibernation. They hardly breathe, and their hearts beat very slowly. They use little energy. Groundhogs retreat to their burrows to hibernate in autumn. Strangely, all groundhogs wake up on about the same day, usually on February 2.

Getting a Move On

Mammals move around in many different ways. Some creep along quite slowly. Others swim, fly, hop, or run at great speed.

In African grasslands, cheetahs race along at up to 59 miles per hour (95 kmh). Kangaroos are the fastest mammals on two legs—they are champion hoppers. Killer whales are fastest in the oceans. They swim at speeds of up to 34 miles per hour (55 kmh).

▲ Verreaux's sifaka, a type of lemur, is equally agile in the trees and on the ground.

◀ In the tropical forests of South America, sloths spend long hours sleeping. They move very little. Tiny plants called algae grow in their fur and give it a green color.

◄ Flying squirrels cannot really fly, but they have furry flaps of skin between their front and hind legs that they use for gliding. The outstretched skin acts as a parachute, allowing the squirrel to swoop from tree to tree.

Bats are the only mammals that can truly fly. They glide through the air on skin-covered wings, looking for insects or sweet nectar to eat. Bats are nocturnal—they are awake at night. They spend the daylight hours asleep hanging upside-down.

ALL KINDS OF FEET

Mammals have differently shaped feet that help them to move around in their surroundings. Elephants have pillarlike legs and feet to support their great weight. A sloth's curved claws are ideal for hooking around branches. Moles have front feet shaped like shovels, which help them burrow through soil.

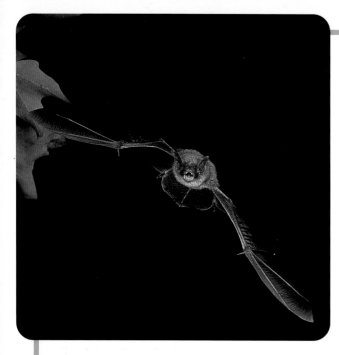

INCREDIBLE SENSES

Mammals experience the world around them using their senses. The five main senses are sight, hearing, smell, taste, and touch.

▲ A little brown bat swoops among the branches, guided by echolocation.

Humans most often use sight to find out about their surroundings. Dogs, foxes, and wolves rely on their keen senses of hearing and smell instead. A bloodhound can track someone down just by following the smell of his or her footprints.

Bushbabies are small, monkeylike creatures. They live in the forests of Africa. Their huge eyes and large, sensitive ears help them to catch flying insects even in dim light.

◄ Like apes, monkeys, and humans, bushbabies see in color. Most other mammals probably see in black and white.

KEEN HEARING

Many mammals have keen sight and hearing to alert them to the danger of predators. Jackrabbits listen for enemies with large ears that turn a round to pinpoint sounds. Mammals are the only animals to have ears placed on the outside of their heads. Lions can turn their ears in different directions to pick up sounds when they hunt.

Sight is a lot less important to other mammals who hunt in darkness or in murky water. Bats and dolphins use an amazing super-sense called **echolocation** to catch their prey. They make high-pitched sounds when they are hunting. These sounds bounce off animals close by, and the bat or dolphin can hear the returning echo. This helps them to find their prey. Echolocation also helps bats to move around easily in the dark.

In Australia, duck-billed platypuses hunt in muddy streams and rivers. They search for worms, fish, and insects with their extremely sensitive bills, or beaks.

▼ The duck-billed platypus uses its amazing beak to sense tiny electrical charges given off by swimming creatures. This mammal looks so weird that when the first platypuses were brought to Europe, experts thought they were fakes.

A Bite to Eat

Mammals need to eat a lot of food just to keep going. Many, including cows, deer, and rabbits, are plant eaters, or herbivores. Others are fierce meat-eating hunters, or carnivores, and they kill animals for food.

Giraffes, the tallest mammals, are plant eaters. They use their long necks to reach up and pluck tender leaves from tall trees. Leaves, grass, and other plant foods are not very nourishing, so giraffes and other plant-eating mammals have to spend a lot of time feeding just to stay alive.

Most animals eat either plants or animals, but pigs, bears, chimpanzees, and humans can eat both. They are called omnivores.

◀ A few types of mammals are bold and powerful enough to kill a person. The tiger is one such animal.

◀ The aye-aye is a strange lemur from the woods of Madagascar, an island off the southeast coast of Africa. It has an extra-long, thin middle finger that it uses to hook out juicy insects from under tree bark.

▶ Giraffes are extraordinary creatures with incredibly long necks, slender legs, and mottled coloring. The first Europeans to see them in Africa could hardly believe their eyes.

Many meat-eating mammals have special colors and markings on their fur that help them hide in their natural surroundings. This is called camouflage, or disguise, and means the hunting animal can creep up on its prey without being seen. In a zoo, a tiger's black-and-orange coat may stand out and look tigerlike, but the same stripes conceal the big cat in its jungle home.

WHAT'S ON THE MENU?

All kinds of creatures are hunted by mammals. Big cats such as lions and tigers prey on other mammals and birds, too. Shrews and hedgehogs eat worms and insects. Marsh mongooses hunt crabs, fish, frogs, and snakes.

Keeping Safe

Many mammals have lots of enemies in the wild—including other mammals. They must be alert to escape possible attackers. Some swim, hop, or run away as quickly as possible. Others have secret weapons or tricks that they use to escape or hide from their enemies.

▼ The porcupine's prickly spines protect it from predators.

Many mammals use camouflage to help them blend in with their surroundings and hide from danger. A zebra's stripes hide it among the grasses of the African plains. A deer's spotted coat helps conceal it in shady woods.

 **THE EYES HAVE IT**

The position of a mammal's eyes can tell you if it is a creature that hunts or one that is hunted. Deer and rabbits, for example, have eyes set on the sides of their heads, so they can spot danger from all around. Predators, such as cats, have eyes that look forward so they can focus and pounce on their prey.

▶ The armadillo is built like a tank, with a covering of tough, bony plates all over its upper body. When threatened, it rolls into a ball to protect its soft belly.

Some mammals have natural armor that protects them when they are threatened. Porcupines and hedgehogs are covered with sharp spines. When cornered, the porcupine turns the sharp spikes on its back toward its enemy and backs away! But a hedgehog in a tight spot rolls itself into a spiny ball. Hedgehogs are found in Europe, Asia, and Africa.

◀ The Virginia opossum has a clever trick to get out of trouble. If a predator spots it, it drops to the ground and lies still, playing dead. Most predators will not touch dead animals, so they move on.

PRODUCING BABIES

Like other animals, one of the main goals in a mammal's life is to produce young. Most baby mammals develop inside their mother's body. There are a few strange animals who produce young in other ways.

In the breeding season, male and female mammals meet to mate. Many males create special areas called territories, where they show off to the opposite sex. Some males get into terrible battles with their rivals to find out who is strongest. Only the winners get the chance to mate.

▲ This female tenrec has an unusually large litter, or group of young. She can rear up to 24 young. Tenrecs live on the island of Madagascar.

▶ Male hippos fight for the right to mate and lead the herd of females. Rivals open their jaws wide to frighten one another. Then they lunge forward and attack their opponent with their teeth.

▲ The female echidna lays a single leathery egg that develops inside a skin pouch on her belly. The baby hatches after about ten days.

GROWING INTO A BABY

Baby mammals spend different amounts of time in the womb before they are ready to be born. This time is called **gestation**. Mice take less than three weeks to grow; humans take nine months. Asian elephants take over 20 months, the longest time of all.

Most baby mammals develop inside their mother's womb, where they are fed by an organ called the placenta. They are born fully formed. The group of marsupials that includes kangaroos develop in a different way. The baby kangaroo is born early, when it is still tiny and unfinished. It crawls up into the warm pouch on its mother's belly, where it finishes growing.

A third, small group of mammals called monotremes have even more unusual breeding habits. They lay eggs instead of giving birth to live babies like other mammals. Of 4,000 different mammals, only three are monotremes: the platypus and two species of echidnas.

GROWING UP

Most animals don't look after their young. They just lay their eggs and leave. When they are born, the new babies can look after themselves. Mammals are different. Many spend weeks or even years raising their young. Parents help them to learn skills they will need in adult life.

▼ This baby kangaroo, or joey, is finishing its development in its mother's pouch.

Mammals are the only animals that produce food for their babies from their own bodies. All baby mammals feed on their mother's milk. The milk contains all the nourishment that the baby needs.

► Mouse opossums are South American marsupials. Females give birth to about ten tiny, helpless babies. They continue to grow in their mother's pouch and later ride around on her back.

▲ **These young red fox cubs are play-fighting. This helps them to grow stronger and teaches them hunting skills.**

At birth, some mammal babies, such as mice, are bald, blind, and helpless. Others, including newborn lambs and calves, are furry and can stand and walk right away.

Baby mammals are born knowing how to do certain things, such as drink their mother's milk. Other skills have to be learned. The young learn hunting and other skills by watching their parents and by practicing. Playing with brothers and sisters also helps to strengthen muscles and develop hunting skills.

TIME TO GROW UP

Small mammals, such as mice, produce many babies that grow up very quickly. In just a few weeks, the young are fully grown and able to produce babies themselves. Larger mammals have fewer babies that grow up much more slowly. Human children take the longest time of all to grow up, perhaps because we have so much to learn.

Happy Families

Some mammals live alone, except when the females are raising babies. Others spend most or all of their lives in a group.

Group life provides safety for all kinds of mammals, especially those that are hunted by predators. On the grasslands of Africa, zebras and antelopes live in big herds. While the herd is grazing, each animal looks up from time to time to check for danger. It warns the others if it sees a threat approaching. Then the whole herd gallops off.

▼ Young elephants grow up in a herd. There are about ten closely related females and their babies. Aunts and grown-up cousins help with baby care. Females stay with the herd when they grow up. Males leave to join a small group of males or live on their own.

▲ Dolphins live and hunt in a group called a school. They whistle to one another to organize their movements as they spread out to surround a shoal, or large group, of fish.

▲ Meerkats live in large underground colonies. To watch for danger, they rear right up on their back legs.

WHAT'S IN A NAME?

Mammal groups have different names. A group of lions is called a pride. Killer whales hunt in a pod, dolphins in a school. Monkeys live in troupes. Bats roost in colonies. Can you find out any other names of mammal groups?

Among lions, wolves, and dolphins, the group is also a hunting party. Group members work together to hunt faster or larger prey than they could on their own. It is mainly female lions who do the hunting. African hunting dogs band together to tackle prey as large as zebras and wildebeest.

Mammals in Danger

A mountain gorilla sleeps in the grass in a forest in Rwanda. Mountain gorillas are in danger of dying out because they are hunted by people.

Wild mammals face many natural dangers, including storms, droughts, and predators. Today, however, the biggest danger comes from human beings. Some of the weirdest, wildest mammals are now in danger of dying out altogether, mainly because of humans.

For centuries, people have hunted mammals, such as whales, deer, and buffalo, for meat. Cheetahs and other big cats have been shot for their beautiful skins. Wild mammals like rhinos and tigers have been killed because people think they are dangerous. Now many of these amazing creatures are very rare.

HABITAT DESTRUCTION

Humans often destroy the homes of other mammals when they clear forests and grasslands to build new towns and roads. As more and more natural places are destroyed there is less and less space for wild mammals to live safely. This is called habitat destruction.

Today, more people are starting to care that beautiful mammals, such as pandas and gorillas, may die out altogether. All over the world, parks and preserves have been set up to help them survive.

Some rare mammals have been bred in zoos and then released into the wild. You can help by sponsoring a rare mammal or joining a conservation group. See page 31.

▶ **Giant pandas live in remote mountain forests in China. They are now very scarce in the wild.**

FACTS ABOUT WEIRD MAMMALS

The blue whale

This giant whale is the world's largest mammal. A big blue whale weighs 150 tons and may be 105 feet (32 m) long. Female whales grow bigger than the males.

Elephants

These are the largest land mammals, standing up to 11.5 feet (3.5 m) high and weighing up to 6.6 tons. The rhinoceros is the second-largest mammal found on land.

Giraffes

These long-necked animals are the world's tallest mammals, towering up to 19 feet (5.8 m). They strip the tender leaves from the acacias and scrub that grow in Africa.

Kitti's hog-nosed bat

This bat is the world's smallest mammal and comes from Thailand. The tiny creature weighs just 0.07 ounce (2 g) and has a wingspan of 6 inches (15 cm). Its body is the size of a bumblebee.

Polar bears

The skin of the polar bear is actually black. This is because black absorbs heat better than paler colors, and allows the bear to get some heat from the Arctic sun.

▼ **Walrus are the heaviest members of the seal family. Big males weigh up to 3,527 pounds (1600 kg). Both sexes have long tusks.**

Siberian tigers

These are the world's largest cats, measuring up to 10 feet (3.15 m) long from the nose to the tip of the tail. Unfortunately, these beautiful mammals are now very rare.

Giant primates

Gorillas are the largest primates—members of the ape and monkey group that includes humans. A male lowland gorilla stands up to 6 feet (1.8 m) tall, shorter than the tallest human, but weighs up to 386 pounds (175 kg).

South American capybara

This is the world's largest rodent (the mammal group that includes rats, mice, and squirrels). It grows up to 4.6 feet (1.4 m) long. The northern pygmy mouse from North America is one of the smallest rodents.

▶ Mandrills are large, heavy monkeys from Africa. Only the male has bright colors on his nose and cheeks.

Speedy cheetah

The cheetah is the fastest short-distance runner. But it tires quite quickly. This large cat puts on a burst of speed to overtake prey.

The three-toed sloth

This odd creature comes from South America and is the world's slowest mammal. It spends four-fifths of its life sleeping.

Humans

Humans live longer than any other mammals, sometimes reaching ages of 105 or more.

Giant anteater

This creature has a very long tongue—up to 24 inches (60 cm) long. It uses it to slurp up ants and termites, and eats up to 30,000 insects a day.

Sperm whales

These whales hold the record as the deepest divers among mammals. These large whales are thought to descend to depths of 9,843 feet (3000 m) when hunting deep-sea prey.

Arctic ground squirrels

These animals spend longer in hibernation than any other mammal. In icy northern lands they spend up to nine months asleep.

WORDS ABOUT WEIRD MAMMALS

blubber (BLUH-bur)
A fatty layer found under the skin of some mammals, such as seals and whales. It keeps them warm in cold water.

camouflage (KAM-uh-flahzh)
The colors and patterns on a mammal's fur that help it to blend in with everything around it. This way it can hide from enemies or sneak up on its prey.

carnivore (KAR-nuh-vor)
An animal that eats the flesh of other animals.

▼ Tasmanian devils are marsupials from the island of Tasmania, south of Australia. They are mainly active at night.

echolocation (ek-oh-loh-KAY-shuhn)
Bats use high-pitched sounds when they hunt. The sounds bounce off animals close by and echo back to the bat. This way the bat can find its prey.

gestation (je-STAY-shuhn)
The carrying of the young.

habitat (HAB-uh-tat)
The particular place where a mammal lives, such as a jungle or a desert.

hatch (hach)
When a fully developed baby animal breaks out of its shell.

herbivore (HUR-bur-vor)
An animal that eats plants.

hibernation (HYE-bur-na-shuhn)
Almost a deathlike state that allows mammals to survive the winter cold. It involves a complete physical change including heartbeat, breathing, and lower body temperature.

litter (LIT-ur)
A group of young all born to a female mammal at once.

mammal (MAM-uhl)
One of the group of animals that have a bony skeleton, fur on their bodies, and glands that produce milk for the young to feed on.

marsupial (mar-SOO-pee-uhl)
One of a group of mammals whose young are born at a very early stage and finish developing in their mother's pouch.

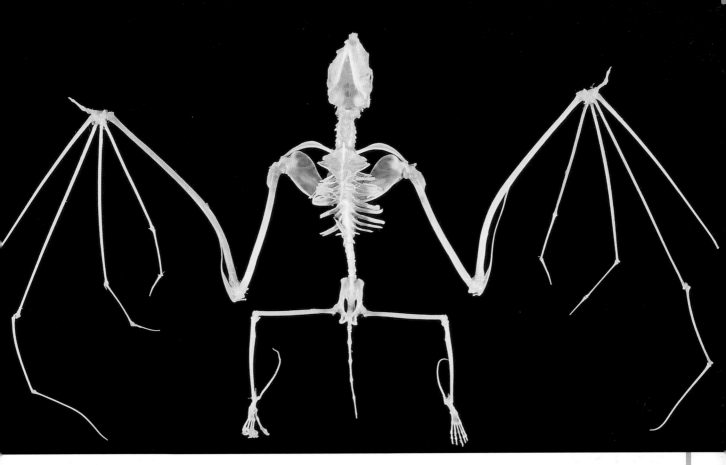

▲ Like all mammals, bats have a bony skeleton to support their bodies.

monotreme (MON-uh-treem)
One of a small group of mammals that lay eggs instead of giving birth to live young.

nocturnal (nok-TUR-nuhl)
An animal that rests by day and is active at night.

predator (PRED-uh-tur)
An animal, such as a tiger or leopard, that catches and kills other animals for food.

prey (pray)
An animal that is hunted for food, such as a rabbit that is hunted by eagles.

primate (PRYE-mate)
A member of the group of mammals that includes apes, monkeys, and humans.

rodent (ROHD-uhnt)
One of the large group of mammals that have chisel-shaped front teeth designed for gnawing plants.

skeleton (SKEL-uh-tuhn)
The bony framework that supports the bodies of animals, such as mammals and birds.

species (SPEE-sheez)
A particular type of animal. The duck-billed platypus is a species of mammal. There are about 4,000 different species of mammals in all.

sponsor (SPON-sur)
To pay for something, usually for a good cause. If you sponsor a rare mammal, you will be helping its species survive.

warm-blooded (WORM-BLUHD-id)
Describes an animal whose body temperature stays about the same, whatever the temperature of its surroundings. Mammals and birds are warm-blooded animals.

How to Spot Weird Mammals

The countryside and even the city where you live is home to all kinds of mammals. Get to know the species in your area by using these hints and tips.

A guidebook of local wildlife will give you details of the mammals that live locally. Some are out and about by day. Others only emerge to look for food at night.

MAMMAL WATCHING

Wear warm, waterproof clothing, in dull colors if possible, when you go mammal watching. Always take an adult with you to keep you safe. Binoculars will help you to study distant mammals. A camping mat will keep you dry on the ground.

▼ These children are mammal watching with an adult.

Wild mammals are naturally shy and will run away if they see you. Approach them downwind (with the wind blowing in your face) so they don't pick up your scent. Move slowly and carefully. The best way to study mammals is to hide behind a tree or bush, and keep very still and quiet!

Find out about local mammals by looking for clues they leave behind them—tufts of hair caught on barbed wire, bones, and droppings. Look out for paw prints in wet soil, by the riverbank, or in fresh snow. Your guidebook will help you to identify the mammals that left them.

Some of the weirdest mammals featured in this book may not live in your local area. The best way to see them may be to visit a zoo.

You can also study how mammals behave by watching your pets, or just look in the mirror!

▲ **A mother cat carries one of her kittens by holding it gently in her mouth.**

CONSERVATION GROUPS

World Wildlife Fund Website

www.worldwildlife.org/fun/kids.cfm
Kid's Stuff page gives fun activities to learn more about protecting animals and our planet.

MAMMAL WEBSITES

If you have access to the Internet, there are lots of websites where you can try to find out more about mammals.

Websites change from time to time, so don't worry if you can't find some of these. You can search for sites with your favorite mammals using any search engine. Include the mammal's scientific (Latin) name if you know it, to narrow your search.

WWF's endangered species page for rare mammals:
www.worldwildlife.org/endangered species

Animal Planet
www.animal.discovery.mammals

Smithsonian National Museum of Natural History, Division of Mammals
www.mnh.si.edu/museum/VirtualTour/ vttemp.html
Take a Virtual Tour of the mammal exhibitions at the Smithsonian National Museum.

INDEX